P9-CDT-732

Media Center

	DATE DUE		

CUTLER MIDDLE SCHOOL

MEDIA CENTER

MEGAN FOX

Maggie Murphy

PowerKiDS
press.
New York

To my editor, Jennifer

Published in 2011 by The Rosen Publishing Group, Inc.
29 East 21st Street, New York, NY 10010

First Edition

Editor: Jennifer Way
Book Design: Kate Laczynski

Photo Credits: Cover Jon Kopaloff/FilmMagic/Getty Images; pp. 5, 11 (top, bottom) Evar
Agostini/Getty Images; p. 7 Jeffrey Mayer/WireImage/Getty Images; p. 8 Vince Bucci/
Getty Images; p. 9 Katy Winn/Getty Images; pp. 10, 20, 21, 25, 26 Kevin Winter/Gett
Images; pp. 12–13 © Buena Vista/courtesy of Everett Collection; pp. 14, 15 Trish Lease/
Getty Images; p. 16 Peter Kramer/Getty Images; p. 17 © DreamWorks/Zuma Press; p. 1
Sergio Dionisio/Getty Images; p. 19 Shutterstock.com; p. 23 © Paramount Pictures/Zumc
Press; p. 24 Toshifumi Kitamura/AFP/Getty Images; p. 27 Jason Merritt/Getty Images;
pp. 28, 30 Frazer Harrison/Getty Images; p. 29 Michael Buckner/Getty Images for GQ.

Library of Congress Cataloging-in-Publication Data

Murphy, Maggie.
 Megan Fox / by Maggie Murphy. — 1st ed.
    p. cm. — (Movie superstars)
 Includes webliography and index.
 ISBN 978-1-4488-2567-7 (library binding) — ISBN 978-1-4488-2723-7 (pbk.) —
 ISBN 978-1-4488-2724-4 (6-pack)
 1. Fox, Megan, 1986—Juvenile literature. 2. Actors—United States—Biography—Juveni
 literature. I. Title.
 PN2287.F6245M87 2011
 791.4302'8092—dc22
 [B]
                              2010034281

Manufactured in the United States of America

CPSIA Compliance Information: Batch #WW11PK: For Further Information contact Rosen Publishing, New York, New York at 1-800-237-9932

★ Contents

Meet Megan Fox 4

Fox's Childhood 6

Early Roles 8

Drama Queen On the Big Screen 11

Hope & Faith 14

Transformers Star 17

Revenge of the Fallen 21

Other Movies 25

Fox's Awards 27

Family, Friends, and Future 29

Glossary 31

Index 32

Web Sites 32

MEET MEGAN FOX

Megan Fox is an American movie and television actress. Fox is famous for playing Mikaela Banes in the movies *Transformers* and *Transformers: Revenge of the Fallen*. She has acted in several other movies, including *Holiday in the Sun*, *Confessions of a Teenage Drama Queen*, and *Jonah Hex*, as well. Fox is also known for her **role** on a television show called *Hope & Faith*. Fox was born in Tennessee and raised in Tennessee and Florida. She was interested in acting and modeling at an early age. Now, Fox is one of Hollywood's most famous young actresses.

Megan Fox is one of today's most popular actresses. She is best known for her work in the Transformers *movies.*

OAK RIDGE

TENNESSEE

This map shows where Oak Ridge is in the state of Tennessee.

Megan Fox was born on May 16, 1986, in Oak Ridge, Tennessee. She is of French, Irish, and Native American **ancestry**. Fox's parents divorced when she was very young. Her mother remarried, and the family moved to Kingston, Tennessee. Fox knew she wanted to perform for people at a young age. She started taking dance classes when she was five years old. When she was 10, her family moved to Florida. There, she started taking acting and modeling classes at age 13.

Fox has said she grew up listening to classic rock and punk rock music. She also enjoyed reading and drawing comic books.

Here is Megan at age 17. She is at the opening of a movie.

EARLY ROLES

When she was 15, Megan's acting lessons paid off. She got the chance to act in her first movie, *Holiday in the Sun*. *Holiday in the Sun* was a direct-to-DVD movie starring Mary-Kate and Ashley Olsen. The movie was about twin sisters who go on vacation to the Bahamas

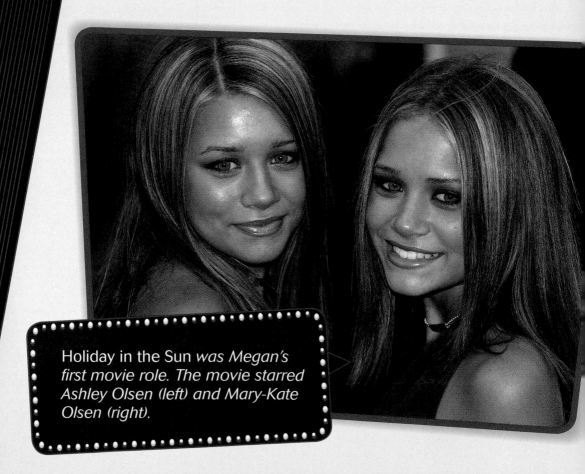

Holiday in the Sun *was Megan's first movie role. The movie starred Ashley Olsen (left) and Mary-Kate Olsen (right).*

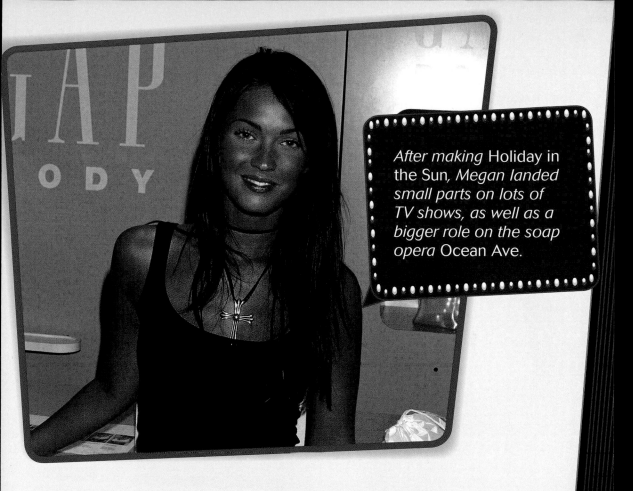

After making Holiday in the Sun, *Megan landed small parts on lots of TV shows, as well as a bigger role on the soap opera* Ocean Ave.

with their parents. Megan played Brianna Wallace, a rich, spoiled girl whom the twins meet on their vacation.

After appearing in *Holiday in the Sun*, Megan played a **recurring** role on a Swedish-American **soap opera** while she lived in Florida. The show was called *Ocean Ave.* Megan appeared in

Martin Lawrence (left) and Will Smith (right) were the stars of Bad Boys II. *Megan was an extra in this movie.*

more than 100 episodes of *Ocean Ave.* between 2002 and 2003. She played a character named Ione Starr.

Megan also played small guest roles on other television shows. She appeared in an episode of *What I Like About You* in 2003 and an episode of *Two and a Half Men* in 2004.

When Megan Fox was 17, she decided to finish high school early. Megan and her mother moved to Los Angeles so Megan could follow her dream to be an actress. Soon, Megan landed a large role in a Disney movie called *Confessions of a Teenage Drama Queen*, starring Lindsay Lohan.

Above: *Here is Megan at the New York City opening of* Confessions of a Teenage Drama Queen. Left: *Lindsay Lohan starred in* Confessions of a Teenage Drama Queen.

Confessions of a Teenage Drama Queen was a comedy about a teenage girl named Lola, played by Lohan. Lola wants to become a famous Broadway theater actress. However, her family moves from New York City, where Broadway theaters are, to suburban New Jersey. Megan played Lola's enemy, Carla Santini. Carla is the most popular girl in Lola's new school. After Lola gets the starring role in their school play, Carla tries to make Lola's life miserable.

In Confessions of a Teenage Drama Queen, *Megan (center) plays a popular girl who is the enemy of Lindsay Lohan's character.*

Confessions of a Teenage Drama Queen opened in theaters in February 2004. Many **critics** gave the movie bad **reviews**. However, Fox got noticed as an actress because of her role as Carla.

HOPE & FAITH

Here is Fox with her Hope & Faith *costars Macey Cruthird (left) and Paulie Litt (center).*

Megan Fox's next major role was on a television show called *Hope & Faith*. *Hope & Faith* was a comedy starring Kelly Ripa and Faith Ford. It was about a soap opera star named Faith, played by Ripa, and her sister, Hope, played by Ford. In the show, Faith moves in with Hope's family after

the character she plays in
the soap opera gets killed
off. Hope and Faith are very
different from each other.
They try to get along without
driving each other crazy, though.

In *Hope & Faith*, Fox played Hope's oldest
daughter, Sydney, during the show's second and
third seasons. A different actress played Sydney

*Ted McGinley
(center) and Faith Ford
(right) played Fox's
character's parents
on* Hope & Faith. *Kelly
Ripa (left) played Faith,
Hope's sister.*

during the first season. Like some of Fox's other movie and television characters, Sydney was a very popular girl who could sometimes be mean to others. Fox played Sydney in 37 episodes between 2004 and 2006. This role brought her more experience as an actress.

Fox played Sydney on Hope & Faith. *Sydney is the oldest of Hope's three children.*

Megan Fox (left) and Shia LaBeouf (right) were costars in Transformers. *They play people caught up in a battle between warring alien robots.*

In July 2007, Megan Fox played a lead role in a movie called *Transformers. Transformers* was a **science-fiction** and action movie about alien robots. *Transformers* was directed by Michael Bay and starred Shia LaBeouf. It also **featured** Josh Duhamel, Tyrese Gibson, and Jon Voight. The idea for the movie came from a line of popular toys from the 1980s.

Mikaela, Fox's character in *Transformers, uses her knowledge of cars to help the Autobots beat the Decepticons. This role brought Fox lots of new fans.*

In *Transformers*, Fox played a character named Mikaela Banes. Mikaela is a teenage girl who knows a lot about cars. She is also the love interest of LaBeouf's character, Sam Witwicky. In *Transformers*, Sam and Mikaela become involved in the battle between two different kinds of alien robots, the good Autobots and the evil Decepticons. These robots can transform themselves into different kinds of machines, such as cars and trucks. Mikaela uses her knowledge of cars to help the Autobots beat the Decepticons.

The Transformers *movies were based on a 1980s cartoon. That cartoon had a toy for each of the characters, like the one shown here.*

Transformers was a very successful movie. It received many good reviews from movie critics. Audiences also loved the movie's action scenes and special effects. Transformers made more than $700 million worldwide. It also won many awards, includin a 2008 MTV Movie Award for Best Movie. Fo quickly became very famous because of her role as Mikaela Banes. The movie brought her many fans.

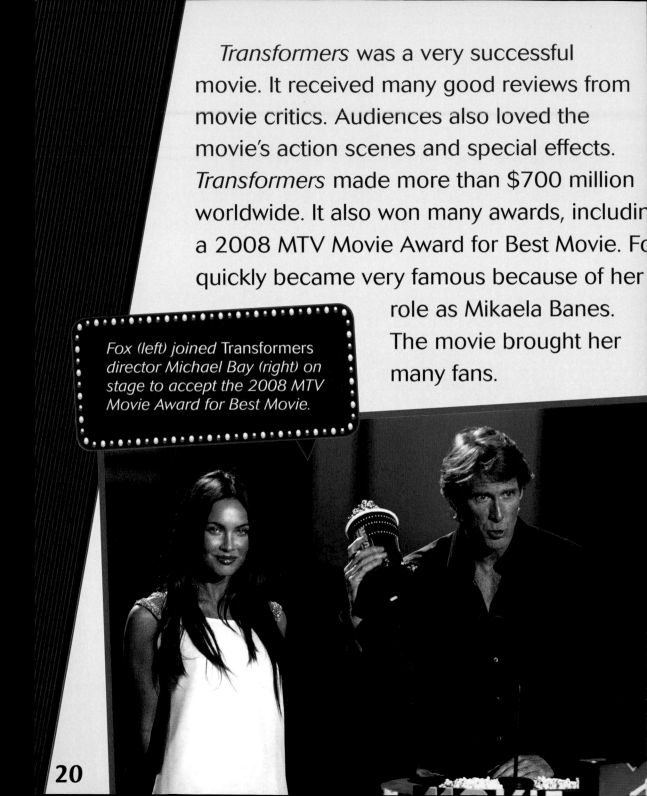

Fox (left) joined Transformers director Michael Bay (right) on stage to accept the 2008 MTV Movie Award for Best Movie.

Megan Fox and Shia LaBeouf have become friends since filming the Transformers *movies.*

Transformers was so successful with audiences and critics that a **sequel** to the movie was made. The sequel was called *Transformers: Revenge of the Fallen*. The sequel was again directed by Michael Bay and starred Shia LaBeouf as Sam Witwicky. It opened in movie theaters in June 2009.

Fox returned in her role as Mikaela Banes in *Transformers: Revenge of the Fallen*. This time Mikaela is Sam's girlfriend. The sequel takes place when Sam is beginning college, two years after the first *Transformers* movie ends. In the movie, Sam and Mikaela must help the good Autobots win another battle against the evil Decepticon robots. The movie features

Fox played Mikaela Banes again in the 2009 movie Transformers: Revenge of the Fallen. *In this movie, Mikaela has become Sam's girlfriend.*

a lot of **stunts**, **computer-generated** action, and exciting special effects.

Transformers: Revenge of the Fallen was very successful with movie audiences. It made $800

SUPERSTAR FACT

Megan Fox is a big fan of comic books and video games.

23

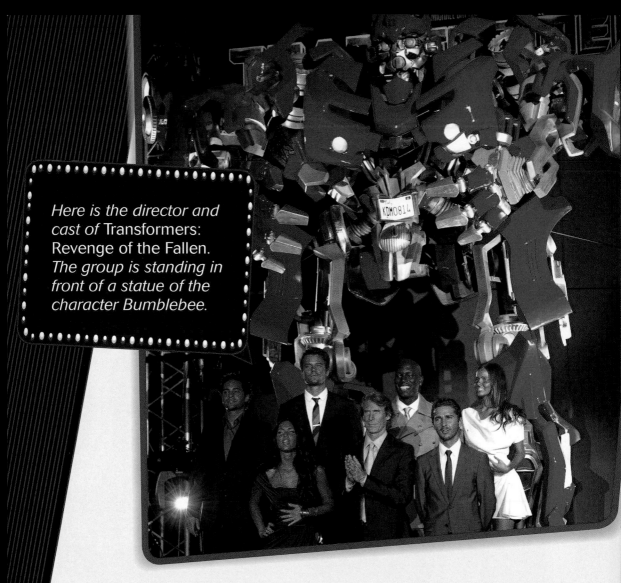

Here is the director and cast of *Transformers: Revenge of the Fallen. The group is standing in front of a statue of the character Bumblebee.*

million worldwide. However, many critics did not like the sequel as much as the first movie. Fox also has said that she was unhappy during the making of *Transformers: Revenge of the Fallen*. She often got into arguments with director Michael Bay. Fox did not return for the third *Transformers* movie.

In the fall of 2009, Megan Fox starred in a horror movie called *Jennifer's Body*. The **script** for *Jennifer's Body* was written by Diablo Cody, who won an Academy Award for her script for the movie *Juno*. *Jennifer's Body* also starred actress Amanda Seyfried. In this movie, Fox played the role of Jennifer, a high-school cheerleader who becomes very evil.

Fox (left) played the lead role in Jennifer's Body, *which was written by Diablo Cody (right).*

In 2010, Fox also appeared in a movie called *Jonah Hex*, starring Josh Brolin and John Malkovich. *Jonah Hex* was based on a comic-book series set in the American West after the **Civil War**. In this movie, Fox played a character named Lilah.

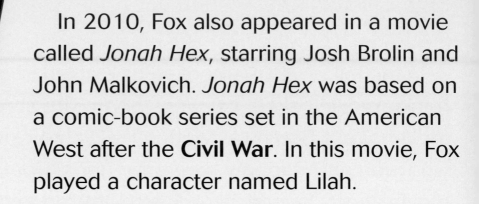

Josh Brolin played the lead in Jonah Hex, *while Fox played a supporting role.*

Fox has been **nominated** for several awards for her acting roles. She has won some awards as well. In 2005, Fox was nominated for a Young Artist Award for her acting in *Hope & Faith*. Then, she was nominated for three Teen Choice Awards in 2007 and an MTV Movie Award in 2008 for her performance in *Transformers*.

Here is Fox posing with one of her two 2009 Teen Choice Awards.

In 2008, Fox won an MTV Movie Award for her role in Transformers.

In 2009, Fox won two Teen Choice Awards after appearing in the *Transformers* sequel. She also won a 2009 Scream Award and a 2009 Spike Video Game Award. In 2010, she was nominated for a Kids' Choice Award and another MTV Movie Award.

Fox is married to actor Brian Austin Green. She is stepmother to Green's son Kassius. She is also good friends with some of the actors she has worked with, such as *Transformers* costar Shia LaBeouf and *Jennifer's Body* costar Amanda Seyfried.

Fox married Brian Austin Green in 2010. The couple had dated off and on since 2004.

29

Here is Fox greeting some of her fans at the Los Angeles opening of Transformers.

In 2011, Fox appeared in a **thriller** called *The Crossing*. She is starting to **produce** movies, too. Fox's fans look forward to seeing what else she will do in the future!

ancestry (AN-ses-tree) The group of people who make up a person's relatives who lived long ago.

Civil War (SIH-vul WOR) The war fought between the Northern and the Southern states of America from 1861 to 1865.

computer-generated (kum-pyoo-ter-JEH-neh-rayt-ed) Made something using computers.

critics (KRIH-tiks) People who write their opinions about things.

featured (FEE-churd) Made an appearance.

nominated (NO-muh-nayt-ed) Suggested that someone or something should be given an award or a position.

produce (pruh-DOOS) To make something.

recurring (rih-KUR-ing) Appearing in a TV show more than once.

reviews (rih-VYOOZ) Written opinions that list something's good and bad points.

role (ROHL) An actor's part in a movie, play, or TV show.

science-fiction (sy-unts-FIK-shun) Work that deals with the effect of real or imagined science.

script (SKRIPT) The written story of a play, movie, radio, or television program.

sequel (SEE-kwel) The next in a series.

soap opera (SOHP O-peh-ruh) A TV show that has ongoing story lines that deal with romantic relationships.

stunts (STUNTS) Acts that need special skills or strength to do.

thriller (THRIH-ler) A movie with action, adventure, and mystery.

★ Index

C
Confessions of a
   Teenage Drama
   Queen, 4, 11–13
critics, 13, 20–21, 24

F
family, 6–7, 12, 14
Florida, 4, 7, 9

H
Holiday in the Sun, 4,
   8–9
Hope & Faith, 4,
   14–15, 27

J
Jonah Hex, 4, 26

M
mother, 6, 11
movie(s), 4, 8, 11,
   13, 17, 20–22,
   24–26, 30

R
reviews, 13, 20
role(s), 4, 9–14,
   16–17, 20, 22,
   25, 27

S
script, 25
sequel, 21–22, 24, 28
show(s), 4, 9–10, 14
soap opera, 9, 15
stunts, 22

T
Tennessee, 4, 6
thriller, 30
Transformers, 4, 17–18,
   20–22, 27
Transformers: Revenge
   of the Fallen, 4,
   21–22, 24

★ Web Sites

Due to the changing nature of Internet links, PowerKids Press has developed an online list of Web sites related to the subject of this book. This site is updated regularly. Please use this link to access the list: www.powerkidslinks.com/mss/mfox/